WRECK THIS JOURNAL

TO ~~CREATE IS TO DESTROY~~ NOW IN COLOR

BY KERI SMITH

PENGUIN BOOKS

PENGUIN BOOKS

AN IMPRINT OF PENGUIN RANDOM HOUSE LLC

375 HUDSON STREET

NEW YORK, NEW YORK 10014

PENGUIN.COM

FIRST PUBLISHED IN THE UNITED STATES OF AMERICA BY PERIGEE,
AN IMPRINT OF PENGUIN GROUP (USA) INC, 2007
EXPANDED EDITION PUBLISHED 2012
PUBLISHED IN PENGUIN BOOKS 2016
THIS EDITION WITH COLOR ILLUSTRATIONS AND OTHER NEW MATERIAL PUBLISHED 2017

ART AND DESIGN BY KERI SMITH

"NOW IN COLOR" EDITION ISBN: 9780143131663
EXPANDED EDITION ISBN (BLACK): 9780399161940
EXPANDED EDITION ISBN (DUCT TAPE): 9780399162701
EXPANDED EDITION ISBN (PAPER BAG): 9780399162718
EXPANDED EDITION ISBN (RED): 9780399162725

THE LIBRARY OF CONGRESS HAS CATALOGED THE ORIGINAL EDITION AS FOLLOWS:
SMITH, KERI.
WRECK THIS JOURNAL : TO CREATE IS TO DESTROY / BY KERI SMITH.
P. CM
ISBN-13: 9780399533464
I. SMITH, KERI. I. TITLE.
NC139.S5665A4   2007
153.35   DC22   2006050329

PRINTED IN THE UNITED STATES OF AMERICA
13

SOME OF THE ACTIVITIES SUGGESTED IN THIS BOOK MAY NOT BE APPROPRIATE FOR
UNSUPERVISED CHILDREN.

18th Printing

WARNING: DURING THE PROCESS OF THIS BOOK, YOU WILL GET DIRTY. YOU MAY FIND YOURSELF COVERED IN PAINT, OR ANY OTHER NUMBER OF FOREIGN SUBSTANCES. YOU WILL GET WET. YOU MAY BE ASKED TO DO THINGS YOU QUESTION. YOU MAY GRIEVE FOR THE PERFECT STATE THAT YOU FOUND THE BOOK IN. YOU MAY BEGIN TO SEE CREATIVE DESTRUCTION EVERYWHERE. YOU MAY BEGIN TO LIVE MORE RECKLESSLY.

NOTE TO THE READER:

FOR THOSE OF YOU WHO HAVE WRECKED BEFORE, YOU'LL FIND SOME FAMILIAR PROMPTS, SOME THAT ARE CLOSE TO FAMILIAR AND SOME THAT ARE TOTALLY NEW. YOUR CHALLENGE HERE IS TO BE AWARE OF COLOR. HOW DOES THINKING ABOUT COLOR AFFECT YOUR WRECKING EXPERIENCE?

INTRODUCTION

YOU MAY BE ASKING, WHY WOULD ANYONE PUT AN INTRODUCTION IN A BOOK THAT IS INTENDED TO BE DESTROYED?

YOU DON'T WANT TO READ SOMETHING IN YOUR WRECK THIS JOURNAL — YOU WANT TO GET STRAIGHT TO THE BUSINESS OF WRECKING. THAT IS WHY YOU ARE HERE, NO?

"DON'T SLOW ME DOWN WITH IDLE CHATTER. I AM HERE TO GET TO WORK."

BUT YOU SEE, I AM HERE BECAUSE WE HAVEN'T TALKED MUCH. AND THERE ARE SOME THINGS THAT I WANT TO TELL YOU. MAYBE THINGS I NEED TO TELL YOU. IMPORTANT THINGS THAT I HAVE TO SHARE WITH YOU ALONE BECAUSE THEY INVOLVE YOU DIRECTLY. IN OTHER WORDS, THIS INTRODUCTION COULDN'T BE HELPED.

IF YOU ARE READING THIS RIGHT NOW, IT MEANS THAT THIS IS A SPECIAL MESSAGE JUST FOR YOU, NOT JUST ANYBODY. ALL BOOKS ARE LIKE THAT; THEY COME TO YOU AT THE EXACT MOMENT YOU MIGHT NEED THEM, OFTEN WHEN THEY ARE LEAST EXPECTED. DO YOU BELIEVE IN FATE? WHAT ABOUT LITERARY HAPPENSTANCE — THAT BOOKS COME TO YOU AT THE PRECISE MOMENT YOU NEED THEM? MAYBE THIS BOOK IS LIKE THAT. IN ANY CASE, I WILL BE BRIEF SO THAT YOU CAN MOVE ON TO THE GOOD STUFF.

IMPORTANT POINT #1

IT HAS BEEN TEN YEARS SINCE WRECK THIS JOURNAL WAS FIRST PUBLISHED. SO MUCH HAS HAPPENED IN THAT TIME. I GET LETTERS EVERY

WEEK FROM PEOPLE TELLING INCREDIBLE STORIES ABOUT HOW THIS BOOK HAS AFFECTED THEM AND CHANGED THEIR LIVES. I DID NOT ANTICIPATE THIS RESPONSE IN THE BEGINNING. I WISH I COULD SAY OTHERWISE, BUT THAT IS THE TRUTH. THIS JOURNAL HAS BECOME VERY IMPORTANT FOR PEOPLE WHO ARE GOING THROUGH EXTREMELY CHALLENGING EXPERIENCES. OR MAYBE FOR PEOPLE WHO ARE JUST LIVING LIFE. THERE IS TOO MUCH FOR ME TO WRITE ABOUT EVERYTHING THAT HAS HAPPENED WITH THIS BOOK. BUT YOU CAN SEE FOR YOURSELF. (JUST GOOGLE "WRECK THIS JOURNAL.") IMAGES SPEAK LOUDER THAN WORDS.

IMPORTANT POINT #2

THIS WRECKING BUSINESS IS MUCH BIGGER THAN YOU THINK. IT TRANSLATES TO MORE THAN DESTROYING PAGES IN A BOOK, IF YOU LET IT. THIS BOOK IS A RESPITE, A RETREAT, A SAFE HAVEN, A FORCE OF NATURE, A CHALLENGE, A VOICE, A RELEASE, AN OUTLET, A SOCIAL PRACTICE, A FRIEND, A PHYSICAL EXPERIENCE, A DARE, A SECRET, A TOOL, A THERAPY, AN EXPLOSION. TRUST ME. IT CAN CHANGE YOUR LIFE. THERE IS SOMETHING ALMOST MYSTICAL ABOUT IT, AND YOU WILL KNOW WHAT I MEAN ONCE YOU BEGIN.

IMPORTANT POINT #3

DO YOU KNOW WHAT PAGE IN <u>WRECK THIS JOURNAL</u> SCARES PEOPLE THE MOST? MAYBE YOU ARE AFRAID OF IT TOO. IT'S THE "CRACK THE SPINE" PAGE. PEOPLE HAVE A REALLY HARD TIME WITH THAT ONE. WHATEVER PAGE YOU FEAR THE MOST IS THE EXACT PAGE THAT YOU NEED TO CONQUER IN ORDER TO PUSH PAST FEARS/PERFECTIONIST TENDENCIES. IT'S TRUE. FIND THE PAGE THAT SCARES YOU.

IMPORTANT POINT #4

WHY COLOR? THE HONEST ANSWER IS THAT I AM AFRAID OF COLOR. THERE. I HAVE SAID IT. I THINK I HAVE BEEN AFRAID OF COLOR FOR A LONG TIME. ALL MY WORK IS ABOUT CONFRONTING THINGS THAT MAKE ME UNCOMFORTABLE, BECAUSE WE WERE TRAINED TO DO THE OPPOSITE, TO AVOID DISCOMFORT. BUT REALLY, THE PLACES WE AVOID ARE ALWAYS THE PLACES WE MOST NEED TO GO. SO HERE WE GO.

HOW DO YOU WORK WITH COLOR (PARTICULARLY IF YOU ARE AFRAID OF IT)? YOU JUST DIVE IN, MUCK ABOUT AND PLAY WITH IT. RELEASE ALL ATTACHMENT TO OUTCOME. DO NOT TRY TO MAKE SOMETHING PRETTY. PRETTY IS A BIT BORING. USE CHANCE. CONNECT WITH THE PART OF YOU THAT IS AN ANGRY, IDIOSYNCRATIC MESS. LET THAT PART OF YOU LOOSE ON THIS BOOK. YOU ARE HERE. YOU EXIST. MAKE/LEAVE A MARK. *&^% IT UP!

READY? IT'S TIME.

1. Carry this with you everywhere you go.

2. Follow the instructions on every page.

3. Order is not important.

4. Instructions are open to interpretation.

5. Experiment. (work against your better judgment.)

6. USE THE COLOR PAGES AT THE BACK OF THE BOOK TO COMPLETE SOME OF THE PROMPTS. CUT THEM UP.

materials

ideas
gum
glue
dirt
saliva
water
weather
garbage
plant life
pencil/pen
needle & thread
stamps
stickers
sticky things
sticks
spoons
comb
twist tie
ink
paint
grass
detergent
grease
tears
crayons

smells
hands
string
ball
unpredictability
spontaneity
photos
newspaper
white things
office supplies
wax
found items
stapler
food
tea/coffee
emotions
fears
shoes
matches
biology
scissors
tape
time
happenstance
gumption
sharp things

ADD YOUR OWN PAGE NUMBERS.

STARTING HERE

CRACK THE SPINE.

COLOR THIS PAGE
RED
ON PURPOSE.

POUR, SPILL, drip, SPIT, fling DIFFERENT COLORED DRINKS HERE.

POKE HOLES IN
THIS PAGE USING
A PENCIL.

DRAW FAT LINES AND THIN.

PUSHING REALLY HARD WITH THE PENCIL.

THIS PAGE IS FOR HANDPRINTS
OR FINGERPRINTS.
GET THEM DIRTY, THEN PRESS DOWN.

COLOR THIS ENTIRE PAGE.

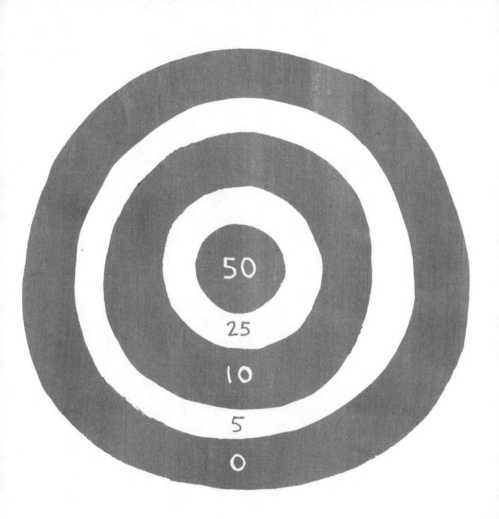

THROW SOMETHING.

A PENCIL, A BALL DIPPED IN PAINT.

PRESS LEAVES AND OTHER FOUND THINGS.

DO SOME RUBBINGS
WITH A PENCIL
CRAYON.

SCRIBBLE WILDLY,
VIOLENTLY, with
RECKLESS ABANDON.

TEAR STRIPS
OF COLOR.
(THEN TRY SOME PLAID.)

FILL THIS PAGE WITH COLORED
CIRCLES. (AS MANY AS YOU CAN FIT.)

Document the colors of your dinner.

RUB, SMEAR, SPLATTER YOUR FOOD.

USE THIS PAGE AS A NAPKIN.

MIX SO MANY
COLORS THEY
TURN TO
MUD.

TEAR OUT CRUMPLE.

MAKE A PAPER AIRPLANE.

WRAP *something*

WITH THIS PAGE.

like
this

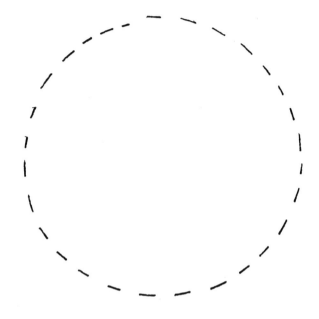

TONGUE PAINTING

1. EAT SOME COLORFUL CANDY.
2. LICK THIS PAGE.

WRITE SOME
THOUGHTS.
COVER UP THESE
THOUGHTS WITH
THE COLOR OF YOUR
CHOICE.

TIE A STRING
TO THE *spine* OF
THIS BOOK.
SWING
WILDLY.
LET IT HIT THE WALLS.

PICK UP THE JOURNAL WITHOUT USING YOUR HANDS.

compost this page.

watch it deteriorate.

DO A really UGLY
(USE UGLY SUBJECT MATTER:
A BADLY DRAWN BIRD,

DRAWING

GUM, POO, DEAD THINGS,
MOLD, BARF, CRUD.)

PRETEND YOU
ARE DOODLING
ON THE BACK
OF AN ENVE-
LOPE WHILE
ON THE PHONE.

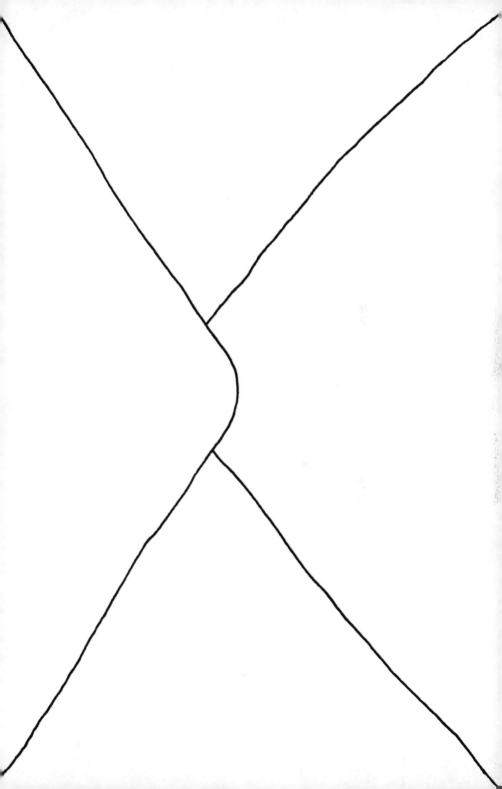

JOURNAL GOLF

1. TEAR OUT PAGE. CRUMPLE INTO A BALL.

2. PLACE JOURNAL INTO A TRIANGLE SHAPE.

3. HIT/KICK THE BALL THROUGH THE TRIANGLE.

make a paper chain.

COLLECT
FRUIT
STICKERS*
HERE.

*STICKERS YOU FIND ON BOUGHT FRUIT.

COVER THIS PAGE

USING ONLY office SUPPLIES.

RUB HERE WITH DIRT.

DRIP
SOMETHING
HERE.
(INK, PAINT, TEA)
CLOSE THE BOOK
TO MAKE A
PRINT.

Sew this page

(with colorful thread or string).

glue A RANDOM PAGE FROM A NEWSPAPER HERE.

ADD COLOR TO IT.

A PLACE FOR YOUR GROCERY LISTS.

CUT UP TINY BITS AND GLUE THEM HERE.

TRACE THE THINGS
IN YOUR BAG (OR POCKETS).
LET THE LINES OVERLAP.

COLLECT THE
COLORS YOU
LIKE HERE.

scribble wildly using only borrowed pens.

(document where they were borrowed from.)

cut strips,
dip them in colors,
glue them back in.

Page of good thoughts.

MAKE PRINTS USING WHATEVER YOU HAVE ON HAND. DIP THINGS IN PAINT, USE AN INK PAD.

ASK A FRIEND
TO DO SOMETHING
DESTRUCTIVE
TO THIS PAGE.
DON'T LOOK.

LET THE COLORS RUN.

GLUE RANDOM
ITEMS HERE.
(i.e., things you find in your
couch, on the street,
etc.)

tear
this
page
out.

PUT IT IN YOUR POCKET.
PUT IT THROUGH THE WASH.
STICK IT BACK IN.

Infuse this page with a smell of your choosing.

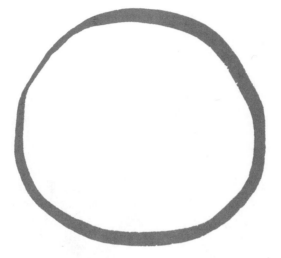

COLOR OUTSIDE
OF THE LINES.

CLOSE YOUR EYES.

CONNECT THE DOTS FROM MEMORY.

COLLECT YOUR

GLUE IT HERE.

↙ ↓ ↓ ↘

POCKET LINT.

1 = BLUE
2 = RED
3 = BLACK
4 = YELLOW

ROLL A DIE TO FIND OUT
WHAT COLOR THIS PAGE
WILL BE.

MAKE DRIPS*

* LIKE JACKSON POLLOCK

SAMPLE VARIOUS SUBSTANCES FOUND IN YOUR HOME.

DOCUMENT WHAT THEY ARE.
CREATE COLOR THEMES.

draw with
SCISSORS.

CUT UP COLOR FROM BACK
OF BOOK AND GLUE IT HERE.

CREATE A DRAWING USING A PIECE (OR SEVERAL PIECES) OF YOUR HAIR.

RESIST!

DRAW WITH A CRAYON,
PAINT OVER TOP.

DRAW <u>LINES</u> USING
WRITING UTENSILS
(STICKS, SPOONS, TWIST TIES,
EVERY TIME YOU CHANGE THE UTENSIL

ABNORMAL
DIPPED IN INK OR PAINT.
COMB, ETC.) CHANGE THE COLOR

PUNCH
THIS
PAGE!
(AFTER DIPPING
YOUR FIST IN
SOMETHING.)

CREATE A COLOR EXPLOSION*

1. TEAR UP SOME COLORED PAPER.
2. COVER PAGE WITH GLUE.
3. DROP PAPER ONTO PAGE.

* LIKE RAUSCHENBERG

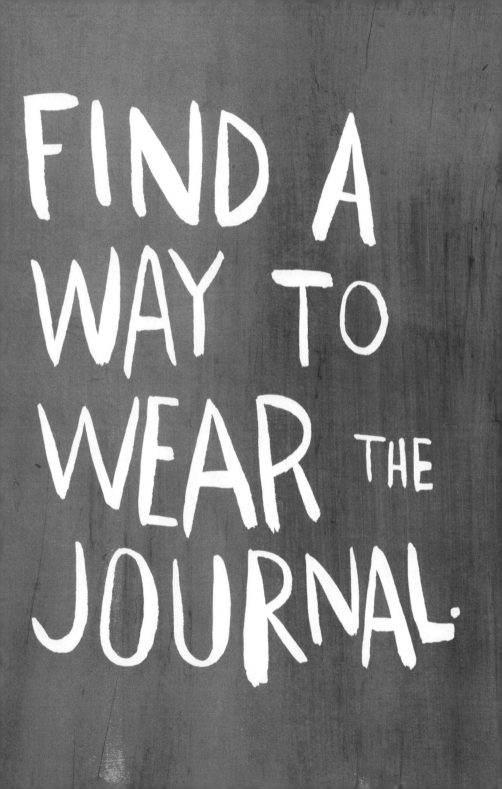

this page is a sign.
what do you want it to say?

CREATE A NONSTOP LINE.

SPACE FOR NEGATIVE COMMENTS.*

(* WHAT IS YOUR INNER CRITIC SAYING?)

MAKE SMUDGES
OF COLOR. RUB
WITH YOUR FINGERS.
ADD WATER.

A PAGE for FOUR-LETTER WORDS.

RANDOMLY CUT OUT SOME
COLORS FROM A MAGAZINE.*
GLUE THEM HERE.

*DO NOT THINK TOO MUCH ABOUT IT.

write with the pen in your mouth.

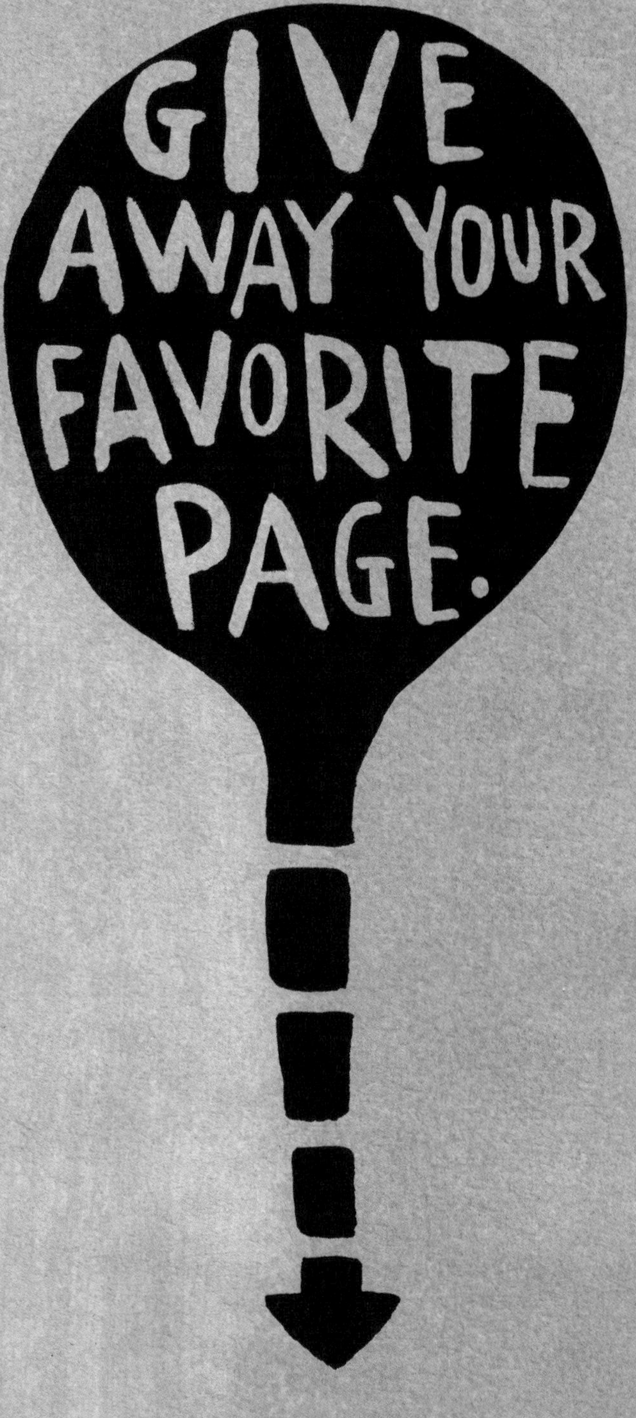
GIVE AWAY YOUR FAVORITE PAGE.

CUT STRIPS.
DO A WEAVING.

DOCUMENT
TIME
PASSING.

HIDE A SECRET MESSAGE SOMEWHERE IN THIS BOOK.

SLEEP WITH THE JOURNAL.

(Describe the experience here.)

CLOSE THE JOURNAL.

WRITE/SCRIBBLE SOMETHING ON THE EDGES.

STAIN LOG

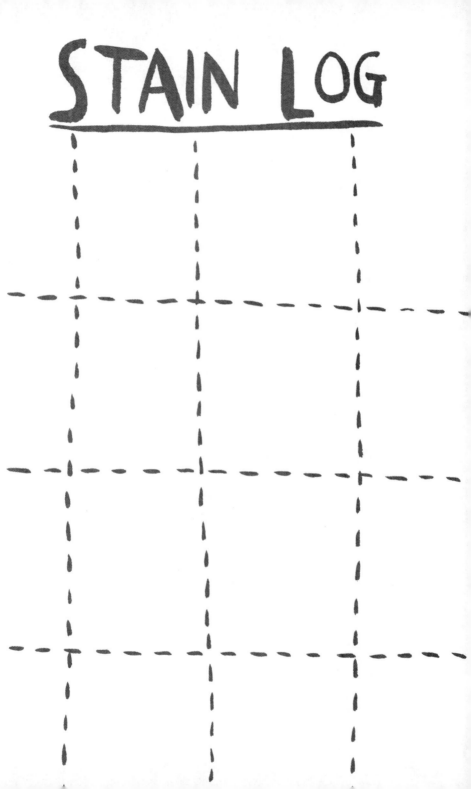

FIGURE OUT A WAY TO ATTACH THESE TWO PAGES TOGETHER.

SPLATTER!

(YES YOU CAN!)

X COLLECT
DEAD
BUGS
HERE.

HIDE THIS PAGE IN
YOUR NEIGHBOR'S
YARD.

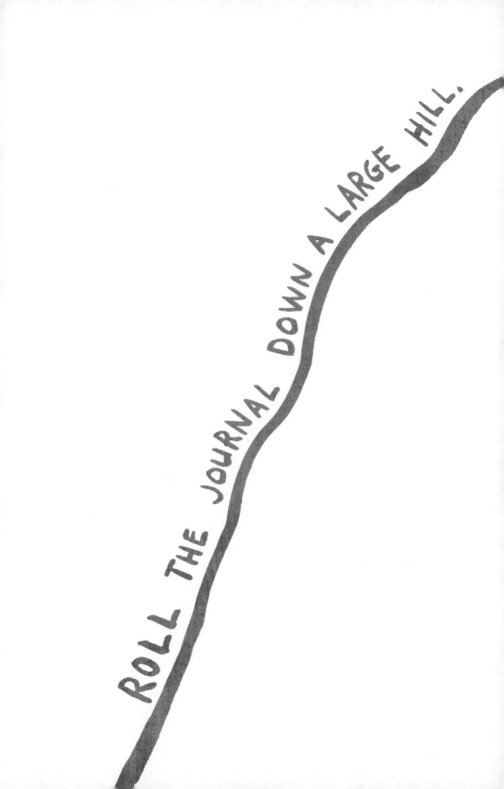

ROLL THE JOURNAL DOWN A LARGE HILL.

SLIDE THE JOURNAL
(THIS PAGE FACEDOWN)
DOWN A LONG HALLWAY.

SQUIRT LIQUID HERE (TRY USING YOUR MOUTH).

COVER THIS PAGE IN TAPE (CREATE SOME KIND OF PATTERN).

1. FOLD THIS PAGE
SEVERAL TIMES.
2. MAKE CUTS WITH
SCISSORS.
3. UNFOLD.

ADD A NEW COLOR TO THIS
PAGE EVERY DAY FOR A MONTH.

7

CUT SLITS*

*LIKE LUCIO FONTANA

FILL IN THESE SHAPES WITH COLOR.*

  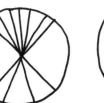           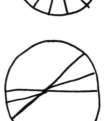

*IF IT LOOKS TOO PRETTY, PLEASE DESTROY.

WRITE A LIST OF MORE WAYS TO
WRECK THIS JOURNAL USING
COLOR AS A TOOL. DO THEM NOW.

1.

2.

3.

4.

5.

6.

7.

8.

9.

10.

11.

ACKNOWLEDGMENTS

THIS BOOK WAS MADE WITH THE HELP OF THE FOLLOWING PEOPLE: MY HUSBAND, JEFFERSON PITCHER, WHO PROVIDES CONSTANT INSPIRATION FOR LIVING A FULL AND DARING LIFE (SOME OF HIS IDEAS ENDED UP HERE). THANKS TO THE TALENTED ARTISTS STEVE LAMBERT AND CYNTHIA YARDLEY. TO MY EDITOR AT PENGUIN, MEG LEDER, WHO EMBRACED AND BELIEVED IN THIS PROJECT FROM THE BEGINNING, YOUR THOUGHTS AND SENSITIVITY LEFT ME WITH SO MUCH GRATITUDE. TO MY AGENT, FAITH HAMLIN, FOR CONTINUING TO BELIEVE IN MY ARTISTIC VISION. TO REBECCA LANDES FOR SHARING HER ARTISTIC HAND. TO CORITA KENT, JOHN CAGE, ROSS MENDES, BRUNO MUNARI, ITALO CALVINO, GEORGES PEREC AND CHARLES AND RAE EAMES. DEDICATED TO PERFECTIONISTS ALL OVER THE WORLD.

PENGUIN
BOOKS